I0818172

ON LONELINESS

How to overcome isolation and enjoy solitude

A photographic project by Julia Hawkins

Published in 2025 by The School of Life
First published in the USA in 2025
930 High Road, London, N12 9RT

Authorised representative in the EEA:
The School of Life Amsterdam, Frederiksplein 54,
1017 XN Amsterdam, Netherlands

Designed and typeset by Marcia Mihotich
Printed in Lithuania by Balto Print

A proportion of this book has appeared online at
www.theschooloflife.com/articles

The School of Life publishes a range of books on essential topics in psychological and emotional life, including relationships, parenting, friendship, careers and fulfilment. The aim is always to help us to understand ourselves better – and thereby to grow calmer, less confused and more purposeful. Discover our full range of titles, including books for children, here:
www.theschooloflife.com/books

The School of Life also offers a comprehensive therapy service, which complements, and draws upon, our published works:
www.theschooloflife.com/therapy

www.theschooloflife.com

ISBN 978-1-916753-21-1

10 9 8 7 6 5 4 3 2

ON LONELINESS

The School of Life

INTRODUCTION

However appalling it may feel, loneliness is – in the end – often an illusion; an unfortunate consequence of not knowing other people well enough. In our isolated hutches, we develop a picture of what our fellow humans are like, which – cruelly – bears little relation to reality. We destroy our self-confidence with repeated convictions that we are the only ones who can feel so many regrets, who are so foolish and so repulsive, who have said so many silly and naïve things, who are so confused and so at sea, so despairing and so hopeful, so worried and so fragile. It's even very difficult – despite every rational reassurance – not to believe, in the end, that we are the only ones without a partner or who will be alone (again) on Saturday night.

In other words, the root cause of loneliness is a lack of reliable information about the true context in which our feelings of isolation unfold; an erroneous fixation that we must be alone in feeling alone.

But nature doesn't create anomalies on the scale we posit. We cannot – on a planet of 8 billion – be as peculiar as we suppose. We never have more in common with others than when we are convinced of our isolation. If only we could believe that, right now, the famous person is lonely, the distinguished person is lonely, the beautiful person without any apparent problems is lonely. The person writing this, and the one reading it, are lonely. This one can't find a way to tell the world who they are sexually; that one never asks for help because they fear rejection. This one, who weeps every night, wears a convincing smile every day; that one, who appears strong, suspects everyone is mocking them. If our collected sighs could be heard, they would be the loudest, most sorrowful sound in the universe.

Deep into the 21st century, we remain hopeless at choreographing events that could give us a chance at breaking down the walls. We continue to make do with institutions known as 'parties', through which we manoeuvre with unwieldy enquiries, like animals trying to break into a jar of honey. 'Been doing anything interesting lately?' we grimace. 'Got any plans for the holidays?' We haven't made progress since the Sumerians.

In fairness, at various points in history, a few ambitious people have had a go at rethinking sociability. There were monks and nuns who took themselves away to sublime buildings in the countryside and attempted to create tight communities in which their souls might mingle with those of others under the eyes of a benevolent god. There were aristocratic hosts and hostesses who put on lavish dinners and intellectual salons, and strove to ensure that the ambassador would meet the scientist and the wit could charm the reverend. But none of this has necessarily helped. We may be living in a city of 10 million and still have no one to eat with tonight. We have worlds to offer, and yet most of us would consider ourselves lucky if we died with two good friends to our name.

This is where art may – on a good day – play a role. We sometimes wonder what art might really be for. The claim here is that it accedes to one of its highest functions when it manages to introduce us to one another's interior lives; when it can tell us something of what everyone is really thinking and what we might actually want to say, were we not so inhibited and ashamed; when it functions as the perfect, abstracted friend – the sort we imagine so well and meet so seldom.

Whenever art manages to do this – be it in a film, a novel, a poem or a set of photographs – we tend to register a basic sense of amazement. How astonishing it is to come away thinking that we're perhaps not wholly distinctive after all. Maybe, despite the surface guff, we're all siblings in the most beautiful, releasing and touching of ways; we in Sydney and La Paz, Ennetmoos and Accra, are all somewhat mad, intense, broken, idealistic, desperate and craving. For a moment, we may feel dizzy at the unity of our state; there has been no point to all our years of reserve and suspicion. The whole defensive structure was built in error. We are among friends, always; we live with brothers and sisters and never knew it. The thought threatens to transform everything.

This kind of happiness can be hard to bear. Which is perhaps why, like many essential ideas, it is in the habit of weakening over time. We need constant reminders of its force – and of its revolutionary potential.

This is the purpose of this modest volume of photographs and interviews: to lay before us a representative sample of humanity, in order to rehearse for us, once more, the idea that shyness and under-confidence have no rationale, and that we have every reason, right now, to throw off our shackles and hold out a hand to our similarly tortured, kind, beautiful and complicated neighbours.

It's in the very confession of our sense of isolation that we can find redemption. Once someone has said, 'I'm lonely', there is never any further reason to believe in our singularity; it's probably the most generous utterance of which anyone is capable.

The cause of loneliness is a devilish myth about what it is to be a normal person. We are only ever lacking information – never humanity or a chance at a new friendship.

THE PHOTOGRAPHS

MAI

I've always been shy and reserved. I find solace in being by myself. I find it difficult to socialise with other people, especially people I don't know. There are some people that get energised by being with other people and there are some that get energised by taking time for themselves; I definitely fit into the second category.

Growing up, I felt I wasn't like other people, and noticing the difference would make me feel even more isolated. I didn't like being considered a lonely person. I would put a lot of energy into trying to be more social and outgoing, but it takes a lot of effort to be what you really are not.

The more I've accepted that I simply am an introverted person, the easier it's become to connect with people.

SHANKAR

I have a skin condition called vitiligo. It started with small specks on my chest and face, and then it just became more and more pronounced. When you are a teenager, your body's going through a lot of changes anyway, and I was petrified. I didn't know anyone who had vitiligo – none of my friends did, there were no celebrities I knew of, there was no one else around to guide me.

I felt so uncomfortable in my own body; it was extremely isolating. I'd search the internet for cures. I found an apparently magical cream online and was working weekends to save for it. But then my parents told me it was a con; there just is no cure. The loneliness has improved as I've learned to accept what's really happened to me.

EMM

My multiple sclerosis (MS) is isolating. It's a difficult condition to explain to people because you can't actually see it for the most part. Sometimes people think I'm well and forget all about it. But I can't forget it for a second – it's my life, and that's isolating.

Sometimes I have to cancel plans because I'm too fatigued and can't think straight. I don't think anyone without MS understands, as much as they try to. It's my body that's betrayed me.

When I have to use my walking stick, people often think that I'm faking it. I was once shouted at by a man on the bus because I didn't give up my seat, which was a horrible moment. I often don't feel like I'm entitled to the comfort and help I crave; it's a lonely place to be in.

JONATHAN

I was with Nigel for almost thirty-nine years. He had previously suffered a stroke and I had been his carer for seven years before he passed. In some ways, what is most difficult is no longer being responsible for him – I suddenly have so much time to fill.

It is the quiet that I find most unsettling. You're used to living with another person who constantly makes little sounds. Now, there's just emptiness; the silence of a mausoleum.

JASPER

My degree is so intense that I've found myself in a cycle of skipped meals, endless all-nighters and social disconnection.

Every waking moment, all I can think about is my work and my worry surrounding it. When I lie in bed, I struggle to sleep because my mind is still racing with thoughts about work.

When I talk to my flatmates, all I can think about is my work. I used to see my friends often, but now I've become a recluse.

It makes me think: sure, I could keep going like this and find success in my career, but would it even matter if I hadn't truly lived?

MOJO

Growing up in care is tough. I struggled to find the sense of belonging that's important when you're developing as a child. I learned how to smile, I learned how to attract people with my personality, but I never learned how to really, properly, belong.

No one in my area ever looked like me; no one had dark gums like me, no one had large nostrils like me, no one had afro hair.

Kids were coming in and out of the care home, but no one ever wanted to adopt or foster me. I started to wonder: when's my turn? When is someone going to come in and offer me a home? Those thoughts drove a feeling of loneliness into my DNA; it became part of my identity.

When I eventually met my biological family, I didn't feel as seen as I'd hoped; they seemed totally alienated from me. I spend a lot of time daydreaming about a different life, a better life, and what that might look like, smell like, taste like.

AZRA

I didn't know my father until I was 43 years old. Not knowing who your dad is, not knowing who you are or who you belong to, is hard. I always felt lost, like I was on the sidelines looking in. As a child, I would fantasise a lot; everything was a fairytale. No one understands unless they've been through it.

When we finally met, his face was so familiar – we looked so alike. He showed me the cottage where he grew up in Cornwall. It's right on the edge of a cliff, such a beautiful place. I finally feel at peace there.

MARIE

I started freelancing and, without realising it, I was alone most of the time. Some days, I am able to convince myself that I am a photographer-to-be, but the reality is that I'm just a lonely housewife with a hobby. I have a sense of shame because of the difficulty I have finding clients.

My partner is the breadwinner. He has a proper career. It's not a choice – I wish I had a career too. Both my grandmothers were feminists; they were fiercely independent. I feel like I've let down their dreams.

OLAIDE

I work in the development and construction industry. I grew up on a council estate in a loving and happy family, but my life experience is very different from that of the people I work with. Most of my colleagues come from a different socio-economic background to me, and I've always felt a little different. I try to find commonalities, but when they are few and far between, you have to work extra hard.

My job involves a lot of socialising, which I really enjoy. However, some decisions still happen at the pub, at rugby or on the golf course. When I had my kids, I wanted a better balance, but there's an expectation that you have to go out all the time. I'm a great believer in trying to cement social bonds, but when that's done in the pub and you're thinking, I left at 7 a.m. today and I'm not going to get back to see my kids before they go to bed, you start to feel like you don't belong.

JOSEPH

When I was 27, I became unexpectedly ill, and after spending time in hospital, I had to move back in with my parents. Physically, I couldn't do the things that I used to be able to do, which was quite isolating.

I never really thought about how my friendships would be tested, but I lost a lot of friends during that time. Some people just didn't really know how to deal with it. But other people surprised me in a good way.

I do often wonder whether I would see friends if I didn't get in touch with them first. I think you have to accept that sometimes you have that role in friendships, but I do question if I'm the only proactive one in the friendship.

I don't need some giant declaration of friendship to feel less lonely – it's the small things, like feeling supported when you're struggling, that matter.

NATHAN

Coming out can be a very isolating experience.

Shortly after I told everyone I was gay, I walked into the boys' locker room and became uneasy – it felt like an 'us versus them' sort of thing. Since then, I've gravitated towards friendships with girls; there's less fear of judgement. I was the only openly gay person in my year for a while.

I have had people come out to me in secret, but that makes me feel even more lonely. Why does sexuality still have to be such a secret – and such a source of shame for people?

MAYAS

Being a refugee is hugely lonely. People don't understand what refugees are, what trauma we have been through, how human we are. We don't have names; we're just abstract statistics.

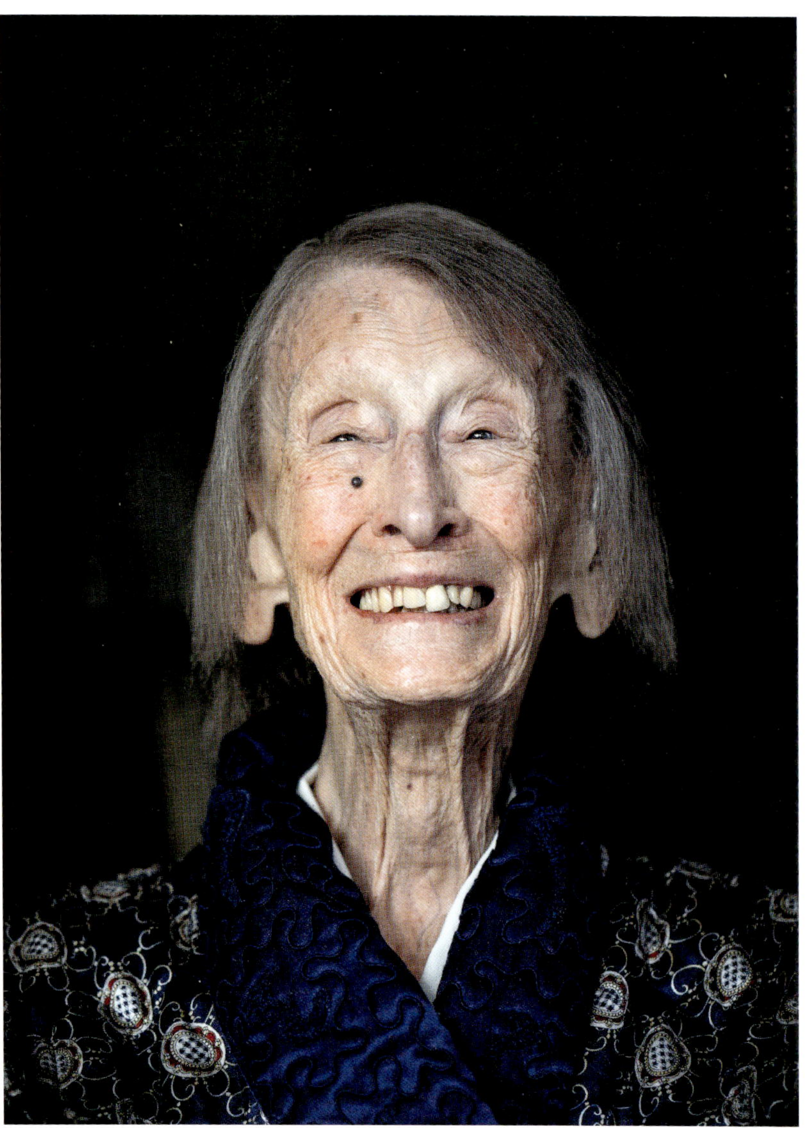

JULIA

I didn't set out to be lonely. I didn't feel lonely when I was little. There were always other children and grown-ups around.

For most of my adult life, I was extremely independent and didn't mind my own company. I travelled all over: the States, China, India – I even saw Mahatma Gandhi!

Now I'm old, loneliness is something very new. My son keeps his eye on me. He does everything for me, which helps tremendously. But I don't like it when he leaves me at home on my own. I feel very isolated then. I hadn't expected this.

NIKE

NOEL

I first went to prison when I was 13 years old. My loneliest memory is going to sleep at night, locked in a room by myself.

From 17 until 22, I went to prison six times. It was awful, but in a sense, I knew my role in prison. It was a home from home in a way.

When my sentence was over, I felt extremely low and isolated, but I couldn't articulate this. I didn't have the tools to do so. It was ironic: I was lonelier free than locked up. I didn't want to be by myself, so I ended up going back to the same places and the same people. I didn't feel I had any other options. I would hang around with bad people so that I didn't feel lonely – to feel part of something, to have a role, to be someone.

Sometimes, people end up committing crime not for the money, but just to stop the ache of loneliness.

RENU

I lost my husband in May 2022. He was diagnosed with prostate cancer in 2019, and at the time we were given three to five years. He had three.

There was chemo, radiotherapy, a lot of gruelling trial therapies. I think I started to feel lonely then because the dynamics of our relationship changed. All of a sudden, the whole focus was on his diagnosis.

I'm a very practical person, and we needed to think about things like wills and funerals, but he wouldn't even acknowledge that we needed to talk about death. Even though he was the one going through the treatment, I felt like I was going through it all with him, and I wanted to be considered as well. At the end of the day, I was the one who was going to be left alone.

After he passed away, I felt like I had to be strong for the people around me, for my son. I didn't feel that I could cry or break down. I think that's when you realise that you're on your own.

BECS

I had wanted to have children, but I was unable to. It was an extremely lonely time, despite being surrounded by caring and compassionate friends. It was an odd kind of loneliness – one accompanied by massive amounts of love.

I had wanted to have children partly to be included by others, to be in their conversations and to explore what they were all going through with their pregnancies. I missed the journey we'd all been on together in our twenties; being at each other's houses, rolling around at festivals and making silly mistakes. Suddenly, they were all going off in a different direction.

I have since made a lot of women friends along the way who aren't mothers, and now my old friends are slowly returning as their children grow older. I had felt isolated for a very long time, even if I never doubted that my friends loved me.

INDIRA

I have a loneliness that comes from straddling different backgrounds. My mum is Indian and my dad is English, and we moved to England when I was 8.

English is my first language, but at school, I was bullied for looking different. I remember one insult: 'Your tongue is too pink.' It's laughable now, but I didn't understand what was happening back then and took it to heart. I look Indian, and I spent half my childhood in India, though I don't speak the language. Sometimes, it's hard to feel fully at ease.

2
Due Date

QUINCE

I often feel like a fish out of water. I've always had different interests from my family and friends, which has isolated me. I'm interested in storytelling, literature, drama, and generally being creative and expressive, but I grew up in an environment that was heavily dominated by men's men, by men being men, and what I care about has never been judged acceptable.

My parents put my sister on a pedestal because she was bright and outgoing, and conformed. I was the opposite – I was withdrawn and insular, and different to my peers.

I'm so aware of not being what others expect me to be.

HALEY

Being a healthcare worker can be lonely because of shift work. It makes your life feel quite itinerant and without consistency.

As I get older, I'm craving the nine-to-five and not having to work weekends. I've missed so many birthdays and weddings because I couldn't get time off from work. It doesn't help you build lasting relationships with people, because you have to cancel and reschedule all the time. That's why a lot of healthcare professionals are friends with other healthcare professionals, so they don't have to explain.

I am aware that it's not healthy to only socialise with people within your profession. You need other inputs, differences, to broaden your horizons.

KATE

I was diagnosed with autism three years ago, and it explained a lot about how different and disconnected I felt from both myself and others. To me, loneliness feels like being lost, invisible. It is a longing to be seen and heard, to be part of the conversation.

For most of my life, connection felt entirely inaccessible to me. I have always loved people, but always felt so separate from every crowd I found myself in. This elusive connection fascinated me; I even made it my job – linking up lonely older people with volunteers for companionship. Facilitating connection for others was the best I could do, and it went some way to satisfying my own need to connect.

My diagnosis has allowed me to be more myself and, interestingly, I have found that I have more in common with others than I had thought, now that I don't mask my true self so much. I spend a lot of time in company these days. I'm fascinated by people, and I love socialising in group settings – which isn't necessarily common for people with autism. I live in a housing cooperative now and feel hugely connected here – working together with the other members of the community to make a home. It feels like I've found my place, at last.

ROBBIE

My girlfriend's faith has been a huge barrier. We've known each other since school. We've grown up together. But her parents didn't approve of our relationship. They suggested that I either convert to Islam or stop wasting her time. They weren't prepared to see me as a real person and tried to isolate me from her. As a result, I didn't see her for two years. It was a very lonely time.

Now we're back together. I genuinely believe that we wouldn't have survived all this if our core beliefs weren't aligned, even if our religions say we are different. We're the same really; two very similar people separated by religion.

DEBBIE

My dad was diagnosed with Alzheimer's twelve years ago. Every time I visit him, I have to introduce myself. The last time I was there, he winked at me. I hope he recognised that I'm somebody familiar. I'd like to think that there are feelings there, but he might act like this with the carers too. They've become as much his family.

As his illness has progressed, we have seen his personality change and start to soften. He never used to talk about his emotions, and then he started to – and would even cry! Who knows what's really going on inside him; I just don't know my own father anymore.

I'm terrified of how lonely he might be feeling, deep within himself.

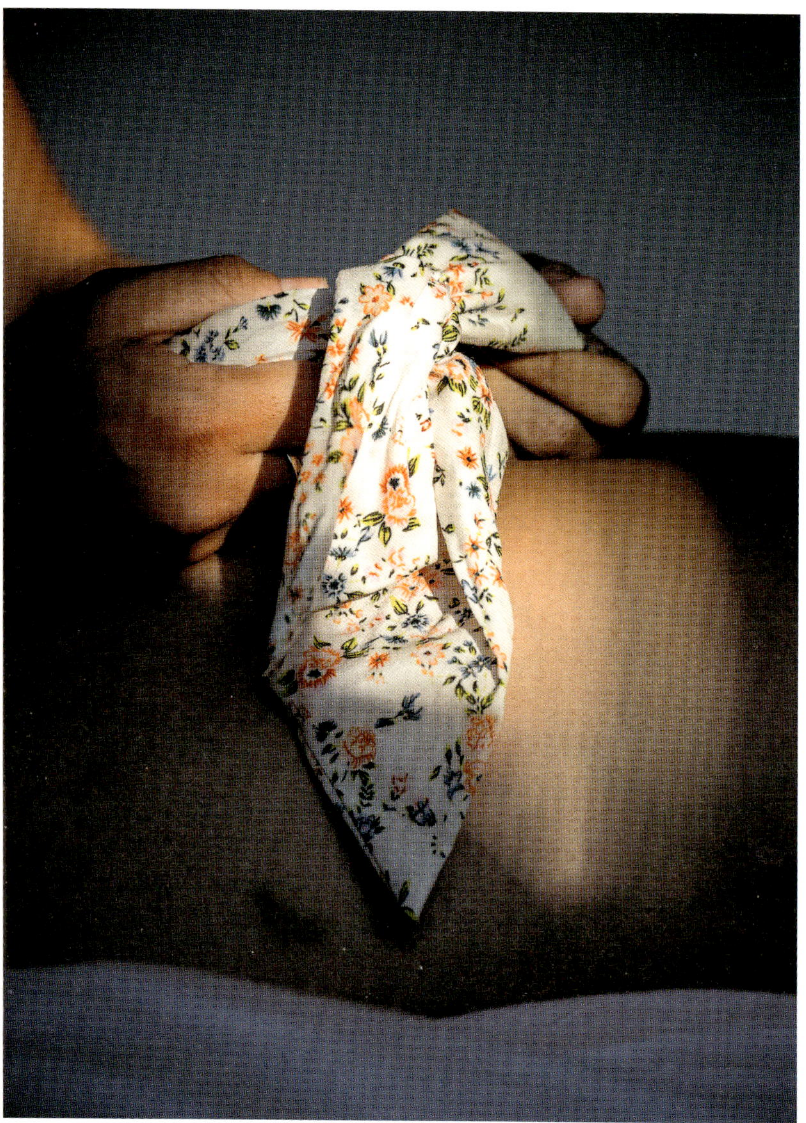

ALLY

One of my closest friends was killed. She was someone who was very involved in my life, and then she was just gone. I found the shock of grief hard.

I tried everything I could to relieve the pain. I sought therapy and was put on anti-anxiety medication because I was having full-blown panic attacks. I was tough on myself when I didn't improve, which made me feel more isolated.

Apparently, shocking and complex grief needs a lot more time than you think. Talking to a colleague who had lost his son helped me feel less alone. He told me that I would need one or two years to even begin to recover, particularly coming up to the anniversary of her death. He said something to me that I loved: 'If it doesn't hurt, they didn't matter. Your pain is a sign of how much she mattered.'

I've got a headband that her family gave me to say thank you. I feel close to her when I wear it.

CLARA

I'm 37 and single. I'm used to distracting myself from feelings of loneliness with work, men and going out. I have been a people pleaser and sought external validation – I've been doing it my whole life. I know that I haven't attracted the right men for me as a result.

Relationships are complicated. You've got to feel good about yourself before meeting anyone.

Recently, I've been trying to sit with and accept my feelings of loneliness. I might put on the television or text my friends and try to distract myself from it as much as I can. It's not always easy, but it's much better than what I had been doing, which was exhausting. I used to see staying in on my own as lazy, that I would never meet someone that way, and I needed to go out and get attention to feel less lonely. But now, I'm trying to be happy in my own company – proving to myself that I can be content. Being at peace with being on my own might just be the best way to eventually find someone worthwhile.

JOHN

I would love to find a significant other. I have never gone on dating apps, but I'm always open to having a partner.

If I try to explain what's happened, maybe it's that I had a very strong relationship with my mum, who passed away in 2008. I sort of think that I was so close to her that she was more or less my significant other for years. My mum was 93 when she passed, so that gives me another ten years. Who knows? It's about living in the now, isn't it?

MAJIKER

I'm aromantic, which means I've never been in, or wanted, a relationship, and I've never experienced romantic love. When I found out that the 'A' in LGBTQIA stood for 'asexual, aromantic or agender' it was a big relief to know that there was nothing wrong with me.

As well as not having romantic partners, I've never wanted to live with anyone, not even in a flat share. I've constructed a life where being on my own is just the norm.

AVA

I don't know anyone as dyslexic as I am; there is no one I can relate to.

It consumes my life and everything I do. I have to take it into consideration when going out with my friends as I need help reading things. I hate it when people have to read the menu for me – but they need to.

Apparently, if you're dyslexic, you have to work eight times harder than normal. People don't realise I need a teaching assistant or technology just to help me read a simple sentence. They say, 'I know other dyslexic people and they don't need that.' Even among dyslexics, I'm not typical!

CORA

I am lonely within my marriage.

We move around the house to avoid each other. I'll often be in the kitchen while he is in his office. I think he must be aware of it.

We went out for a meal for his birthday. I tried to concentrate on what to talk about, to steer a line that didn't get too testing, but it ended up in sniping, as usual. It's very difficult to have a conversation that doesn't degenerate into a full-blown argument.

I've tried unsuccessfully to have conversations with him about where we are going, but he hides from it. I know that if he can't talk, then we can go no further. What is marriage if it's not the opportunity to discuss things? I feel lots of different emotions: angry, frustrated, trapped, desperate …

HANNAH

My eating disorder has completely inhibited how much I socialise, as it affects my ability to relax. The psychology of the disorder is that it persuades you that following its impulses is what's going to make you happy, and nothing else will. It's so convincing that you're determined to get everyone away from you, in case they interfere with what you need to do.

I find it hard to speak to people my own age about it; teenagers don't deal very well with deep, emotional issues. I talk to my mum, but even that is hard as she hasn't struggled herself in this area. Eating disorders are often spoken about as a teenage thing, a phase that will just go away, but when it doesn't, people just don't know what to say. I feel ashamed.

Exit

CAROL

I've lived on this estate for forty-seven years, but people here just don't want to know you. They've got loads of events going on, but I won't go. I went to a party a few weeks ago. I was sitting at the table on my own eating my lunch, while everybody else was sitting in their gangs. It's upsetting when people don't want to talk to you – it makes you feel like you're not wanted. It's like you're not there. My son, Dean, tells me not to worry if nobody talks to me; I should just do my own thing and carry on with the way I am.

My friend Phillippa of ten years meets me once a week and walks me over to the café, where we have a coffee and a pastry. She is a lovely person and always looks after me. She is a godsend. If I don't turn up at the café, they always ask, 'Where is Lady Bling?'

EZEKIEL

I moved, and my friendships just drifted apart. There was a time when I would call friends and hang out, but I don't have that at the moment. I have a lot of acquaintances and people I work with, but my friendship group is non-existent. I look at my phone and there's no one I can call just to have a chat.

I was the firstborn for many years, which meant I spent a lot of time by myself. As a result, I'm very self-sufficient. I never make demands of people because I'm just easy, but on the flip side, I can push friends away because I'm so used to being alone.

I feel lonely almost every day; it comes and goes. I feel like no one would really notice if I weren't here. I need to learn how to make and maintain friendships. I've got so much to learn.

ADEBOWALE

People my age don't talk about loneliness; it's seen as something that makes you look weak. I'm a social person, I go out a lot, but I do feel lonely sometimes. The way that modern society is set up, we are all so separate. There is little community apart from online.

There is no socialising on my university course – we have lectures and then we go home. My dream is for us all to go for a pint and get to know each other. I set up a group chat so that we could talk outside of class and immediately felt part of something, a community. I have suggested going for a drink four times now … No one has replied, so I have left it.

We really need to learn to tie into each other more. I think that would make it much easier to live in this world.

ZOE

It's been three years since I got the diagnosis of young-onset Alzheimer's. I'm at home all day, waiting for everyone to come back, not doing an awful lot. Even though I try to occupy myself – I take the dog for a walk at least twice a day – it never stops the feelings.

I shy away from socialising, even though it's something I have been told you should do, as it's good for your health and wellbeing. I've started to worry about being able to keep up with what people are saying.

There's a group that I'm part of for people with young-onset Alzheimer's. We meet once a month. There's comfort in that.

I have to make the most of it and live my best life, but it can be desperately lonely.

HRISTO

Daniel was my partner for a long time. It was difficult for me to accept when he passed away. I sat on a bench at the hospice and felt like he was sitting next to me. He said, 'I want you to be happy. I want to live this life through you.' Sometimes I wake up in the night and wonder where he is. He isn't there, but I feel him inside.

Through my loneliness, I discovered virtual reality. You can create an avatar and interact with other people. People are not just characters; they express themselves and share their experiences through their avatars. Using virtual reality, I was able to diffuse and process my grief more effectively. Maybe I chose an avatar because Daniel said that he wanted to live through me, and it somehow brought me closer to him.

In a big city like this, people are almost like drones – they have a set life, a set job and set interactions – it can be extremely lonely. Virtual reality has the potential to heal and unite people.

DANIELLE

I came to the UK for a master's degree and chose to stay permanently after securing a job. However, I sometimes question whether it was the right decision.

Despite being surrounded by the people I care about most – my husband and my son – I often feel lonely because I need to communicate with them in English. No matter how hard I try, I still struggle to convey my thoughts effectively.

My son used to speak Chinese fluently before the age of 4, but as English became his first language, his interest in Chinese waned. I try to engage with him in Chinese, but he seems uninterested, and I doubt he understands much of what I'm saying now.

I do meet people and form friendships, but it feels like there's always a barrier that cannot be broken because of cultural differences. You can talk about children and day-to-day life, but a deeper connection is always lacking.

JENNIFER

Akram and I have loneliness in common, but for different reasons. He was born and raised in Palestine, in a community with a very deep sense of place. As a result, he has this baseline level of comfort connecting with other people. For him, there's the loneliness that comes from having to leave that community and uproot himself.

For me, it's the opposite. I never had a sense of home or community. My dad was in the military, and we moved every couple of years. For me, it's almost an existential kind of loneliness; feeling like I don't belong anywhere. There's a sense that, in any group, I am always on the outside looking in. But at least we are not alone in our loneliness and, in a way, having it in common brings us closer.

VAGINA

PINS

The breakdown of a marriage has a long tail. It's lonely, feeling the responsibility of bringing up the kids, trying to make the right decisions about my life and theirs.

The loneliness comes from not having someone to bounce ideas around with, someone to be supportive, and also point out when you're doing something foolish. I talk to friends, and I have lots of people around me whose judgement I trust, but it's different. I feel most alone when I go to bed at night – I've got to face myself and my thoughts.

It always moves me when someone makes me food because I'm so used to making my own. I value it more than I think most people do. I know that food and nurture go together.

Dreams

MAX

I was only 17 when I injured my back during Army training. If you want a picture of loneliness, it's me lying there in absolute silence, unable to move, feeling the tears running down my face.

When you are on benefits, you have no choices. You don't choose where you live, you don't choose what you eat, you certainly don't choose to go on holiday – choices just go. Friends disappear when you physically can't keep up with them and when you're not going to the same clubs or restaurants because you can't afford them. That's why my dog means everything to me. He wants to be next to me all the time – he sleeps in my armpit.

HAYLEY

I was a quiet child. I'd go bright red and lose my words around other people. I coped by shutting down and making myself as small as possible. When I was 19, I attempted suicide because I just didn't see how I could fit in; I didn't feel like I had anything to offer the world. It was a really lonely time.

I have spent a long time learning about introversion and social anxiety, and how that's related to loneliness. Quiet people are often seen as aloof, but perhaps we're just in environments with louder, more dominant people, where it's difficult to break into a conversation. Loneliness is a bit of a warning sign – when we feel lonely, our body starts to shut us down from connection. There are lots of people out there who feel very anxious and lonely, and desperately want connection but don't know how.

I still feel lonely at times, particularly when I find myself standing outside a loved one's 'fortress', trying to find a way in. That said, I've done a lot of work on myself. I've built up my courage and have practised reaching out to others more, creating connections and community in ways that align with my quieter nature.

DAVID

Working remotely often means there's no reason to leave the house, because my work is in the next room. Waking up on a Monday morning, I often think, I am in this house for the next five days, into the weekend. I've started going out for a walk in the morning before work, just to get out of the house.

I have whole days where I am in Zoom meetings. Everything I do seems to be online or on the phone these days, which takes its toll on both your mental and physical health. You hear about supermarkets taking away automated tills because people want to be able to have a conversation with a real person, which I can relate to.

I am actively thinking about closing my business to get a job in an office, within a team. I miss the physical and emotional connection of being in someone else's presence, of their body language, and feeling part of something bigger than just myself.

ELLY

The single mother and only child relationship can be intense. I remember when he was a tiny baby, he was so vulnerable. Now that he is 18, he doesn't need me anymore. You give your all to this person and then they're gone.

Holidays together are something I really miss. He doesn't want to go on holiday with me anymore, which is completely normal at his age. I want him to be happy and do his own thing, but it is hard realising that this is what life is going to be like for me for the foreseeable future. I'm conflicted between feeling liberated and feeling really lonely.

CONNOR

Acting is a lonely profession. I spend an awful lot of time in hotel rooms – fancy, isolated hutches to spend a couple of nights, but I could be there for months. You might be filming on a Monday and then not needed again until Thursday, but you are on standby so you can't go home. You just sit there, day in, day out, with nothing to do and nobody to talk to.

Loneliness, for me, is being away from home; being away from my family. There's a fantastic word in Welsh, *hiraeth*, which means that yearning inside you for home. When the kids were small, the yearning to be at home was unbearable. Being away meant that I missed an awful lot of their childhoods; I missed an awful lot of time with my wife.

When I'm away, I have to be very careful because my immediate response to feeling lonely is to go down the pub, and alcoholism is a problem in my family. I try to read, watch television and walk endlessly instead.

JAKI

I had just got my dream job in a school – my first class as a teacher – when I found a lump in my chest. I had a mastectomy and then chemotherapy for six months, and I had to sign off work for that time.

When I returned, I didn't get my class back. In my absence, they had decided that I would be a cover teacher instead. It was a very lonely period because I felt like I couldn't talk about my disappointment with not being able to continue the role that I had been so excited to start, or what I had just been through. I felt like I had to pretend everything was okay if I wanted to get my class back.

I would come to the allotment to sit and reflect on my experience – to get grounded and reset. The noises here are nice: the fox is about or there's someone rattling the gate coming in. You're with the trees, you've got the birds – you're never lonely here.

ABBEY

I was in my late twenties when I suddenly hit that point – a point I think a lot of women reach – where I felt there was a hole in my life. I needed a baby. But months down the line ... nothing.

We had started down the IVF route when I fell pregnant naturally. But then, I lost it. It was a missed miscarriage – the worst-case scenario after all that time waiting. But I didn't give up and I became pregnant again about six months later. But by that point, the fear had set in. I didn't believe it was going to work out. We went for a scan at around three months, and we were told it had happened again. I could tell by the way they went very quiet during the scan.

It felt like it was all on me. It was so personal that it didn't matter how many people said, 'I'm here for you.' I was alone with my thoughts and a womb that no longer had a baby.

I think even if you have a hugely supportive partner and lots of family around you, any woman going through this experience will have very lonely moments.

DYANA

I'm transitioning from male to female, which is a lifelong journey for some that starts at birth.

I always knew it, but buried it in me because of fear and lack of support in the environment where I grew up. Recently, however, I had new hope again, when I started working as an actor and model during the pandemic. It gave me a lot of joy to be filmed and get the attention of the camera. It really boosted my confidence.

On this journey, I met a photographer, Ana, and we did a collaboration where I had full makeup done. Throughout the process, we ended up talking about transitioning and it was magical. As we become friends, she helped me try on some female clothing in town. I figured out my dress size, and she really helped me to feel confident in shops. On further shoots, we explored that I can actually be quite pretty and feminine.

I thought that if I came out, I would suddenly have a lot of friends, but that's not been the case. I think I naïvely idealised the queer community. I also believe that if I had done this ten or fifteen years ago, I would be part of a group, so it makes me sad. I know it's not just me though. If you look around, there are so many lonely people.

JORDAN

I grew up caring for my brother. He's got additional needs and requires a lot of around-the-clock care. My father hasn't been around for a long time, so my mum had to step up as a single parent and take care of us alone. My older brother, my mother's eldest son, would help a lot, shielding me from any major care responsibilities. I would help in every way I could to make life at home comfortable, like helping out with meals and other chores.

I was always at home or at school. My mum was very protective because we lived in quite a dangerous area of South London, so she always shipped me from home to school, from school to home. I didn't really do anything extra-curricular during my time in primary school – I was a very quiet child. In secondary school, I made attempts to get out of my shell. Joining a school poetry competition helped give me the words to express myself.

When home life gets complicated, everything else gets more complicated. Doing that caregiver role from a young age makes you grow up fast, but it's a useful skill set. I know how to take care of people.

KEALEY

I've always felt quite isolated from my peers.

I was diagnosed with migraines when I was 6 or 7. It's hard to find friends who understand that when I cancel plans, it's not because I'm not interested or don't want to go out – it's just that I always have to think about managing my health.

It can be quite hard being young and having an invisible disability, especially because many older people – or those in positions of power – like to tell me that I'm not working hard enough. But I'm aware of how much strength I have. I find it difficult to give myself recognition, but it's something I've learned to do. And my mum has always instilled in me the importance of being proud of myself.

KEVIN

I think people would describe me as an introvert. I've been on my own for a long time and I enjoy my own company. However, there are times when I recognise feelings of loneliness.

In the world of work, I'm confronted with lots of strangers, and I have to make an effort to be on the same page and get on with everyone. But there are times when I can be quiet, and I think that sometimes gives off an air of not wanting to be involved, though that's not the case, of course. I just find it quite hard to engage with new people.

For me, silence is golden. I think it's beautiful when you and the other person don't feel the need to fill the void with words – when you can just be in the presence of somebody because you want to be with them.

JULIA

(the photographer)

In December 2021, a perfect storm of events – including menopause, a stressful new job and a steroid injection for a frozen shoulder – left me on the floor. I felt more tired than I'd ever done, and my body felt like a lead weight.

I was diagnosed with ME/chronic fatigue syndrome and had to stop work. I spent days lying on the sofa, trying to piece together what had happened. I felt like the 'normal' world had left me behind. I managed to get out most days to my local park and often took my camera with me. I used to sit and watch birds splashing about in the pond. Observing them, trying to find different ways of capturing them, felt so nourishing.

I've slowly built up my strength over the past couple of years. I get out more, and I'm learning to treasure the little things, like being creative, having access to nature and chatting to my lovely neighbours. All of this helps me feel less lonely. But I still feel wistful sometimes when I hear about other people's social lives.

PHOTOGRAPHER BIOGRAPHY

Julia Hawkins creates natural, authentic portraits of people from all walks of life, using her camera to instil a sense of connection and shared humanity. She was a winner of the British Journal of Photography's Portrait of Britain Award in 2024 and was shortlisted for a Be Still Media Prize in the same year.

Julia is a regular contributor to the award-winning *Peckham Peculiar* newspaper and its sister papers, and also works with a range of charities and other purpose-led organisations to help them tell their story in images.

Her career in photography began in 2020 after completing a professional photography course at the London Institute of Photography. Prior to this, she spent more than twenty years working in the non-profit sector, focusing on social and environmental justice.

juliahawkins.com

The photographer would like to thank all the people who have participated in this project, and: Phoebe Adler, Sarah Bell, Debbie Castro, Cathy Deplessis, Tracey Francis, Jim Glennon, Kenny Imafidon MBE, Mark McGinley and Kate White, Alec Leggat, Patrick McLennan, Kirsty McMillan, Holger Pooten, Caterina Nasini, Vicky Ream, Aroona Shawkat and Elahe Ziai. I will be forever grateful.

Also available from The School of Life:

On Divorce

Portraits and voices of separation: a photographic project by Harry Borden

An intimate photographic study on the subject of divorce by Harry Borden and The School of Life.

Everyone wants to talk about weddings; few can bear to consider divorce. But as divorce is the ultimate outcome of around half of all marriages, the topic cries out for fresh consideration and illumination.

This is a visually captivating and psychologically stirring book that restores divorce to its deserved status as a subject of complexity and interest.

Through fourty-eight evocative portraits and poignant interviews by the renowned photographer Harry Borden, readers are introduced to a diverse array of individuals, spanning different ages and backgrounds, whose lives have in some way been impacted by divorce. We hear from children, parents, grandparents and friends; we hear from those who have been devastated by divorce and those who have been saved by divorce; we learn from those who can't bear their exes and a surprising number who have become best friends with them.

The book challenges prevailing clichés and judgements, prejudices and knee-jerk assumptions, leaving readers enlightened, consoled and moved. This is a book for anyone who has ever been through divorce or might somewhere along the line encounter it – that is, for anyone who has ever dared to love.

ISBN: 978-1-915087-39-3

On Family

The joys and challenges of family life; a photographic project

An intimate look at family life through portrait photography and interviews.

Families can be a mystery. Is everyone else's as complicated as ours? Is there such a thing as a 'normal' family? We generally only get to see the polished exteriors and are left to imagine what might be going on behind closed doors.

Here is a book that takes us on a tour around the reality of families. It provides a rare, privileged glimpse into private realms, allowing us a new, profound understanding of ourselves and others.

Comprised of interviews and portraits of over fifty people captured by five supremely talented photographers, it introduces us to an extraordinary array of participants: mothers, fathers, siblings, stepchildren, adoptees, found family, the old and the young.

What surfaces is the astounding diversity of family life – and the number of commonalities, too. Above all, we recognise the fundamental role that family plays in making us who we are.

This is a book for anyone who has ever wondered about their family or fantasised about being part of someone else's. In short, this is a book for us all.

ISBN: 978-1-915087-41-6

Also available from The School of Life:

A Voice of One's Own

A story about confidence and self-belief

A therapeutic novel that teaches us about our own emotions through a young woman's journey of self-discovery.

This is a novel with a striking mission at its heart: not just to tell us a story, but to show us – through the example of one life – how we might change our own. The novel introduces us to Anna, a kind, inspiring, thoughtful but modest and self-questioning person, in whom we might catch echoes of ourselves. Life has been hard of late for Anna: her job is putting her under extreme pressure, her relationship is lacking the support she craves, her parents have saddled her with a complicated emotional history. And yet she is determined to progress and liberate herself from her inhibitions.

In a style that's brief and poignant, accompanied by lyrical and thought-provoking images, we follow Anna as she unpicks the roots of her self-suspicion and discovers something we all deserve but have so often been denied: a voice of our own.

The novel amounts to a bold new kind of fiction: one that doesn't only entertain and move us, but along the way, almost without our noticing, educates and enhances us – nudging us towards new possibilities and courage for ourselves.

ISBN: 978-1-915087-26-3

Confidence in 40 Images

The art of self-belief

An inspiring, curated selection of forty photographs and artworks with accompanying essays, examining the skill of confidence.

The difference between success and failure often comes down to an ingredient that we are seldom directly taught about and may forget to focus on: confidence. What makes one life cheerful, purposeful and energetic and another less so may have nothing to do with intelligence or qualifications; it may simply be bound up with that buoyancy of the heart and mind we call 'confidence'.

Here is a supreme guide to this fatefully neglected quality; a series of encouraging essays that jog us into a new and more fruitful state of mind. The images that accompany the text are included to ensure that we aren't merely intellectually stirred to change our lives, but that we are also given the best kind of visual assistance.

We learn why we should dare to try, why the past doesn't have to dictate the future, why we can alter the way we speak to ourselves and why there are so many reasons to keep faith with our most ambitious aspirations.

ISBN: 978-1-916753-10-5

Also available from The School of Life:

Calm in 40 Images

The art of finding serenity

A soothing gallery of artworks and photography to guide us on a journey towards calm.

Knowing how to be calm deserves to be counted as life's greatest skill, for even if we have every other possible advantage, so long as our mind is frantic, we will never taste the happiness we seek.

This ingenious small book is nothing less than a comprehensive guide to the art of calm. It takes us systematically through the many things that unsettle us and arrives at a range of solutions to ease our spirits and usher in a less fretful and anguished perspective.

Throughout the book, entries are accompanied by images that invite contemplation and generate small moments of joy. We are invited not just to understand calm but to appreciate it with our eyes and discover it with our senses. The book amounts to a small museum of calm and a psychological guidebook that can help to quieten our worries and bring on a new mood of serenity and ease.

ISBN: 978-1-916753-00-6

Self-knowledge in 40 Images

The art of self-understanding

A visual journey to inspire and guide you through the inward exploration of the self.

When Socrates, apparently the wisest man in antiquity, was asked to define our highest purpose as humans, he responded, 'To know ourselves.' The advice has never been bettered. Without self-knowledge, all other efforts will be in vain.

This is a book to help us on our journey to knowing ourselves better. Made up of forty images drawn from across different cultures and eras, it takes us on a tour of certain key ideas that we need in order to befriend our deeper selves. It helps us to understand how our childhoods have shaped us, what difficulties we characteristically experience in relationships and what our purpose should be.

Modern society gives us no shortage of ambitions. We will have landed on the one that can finally bring us peace and freedom when we are ready – with the help of this book – to begin the inward journey.

ISBN: 978-1-915087-42-3

Also available from The School of Life:

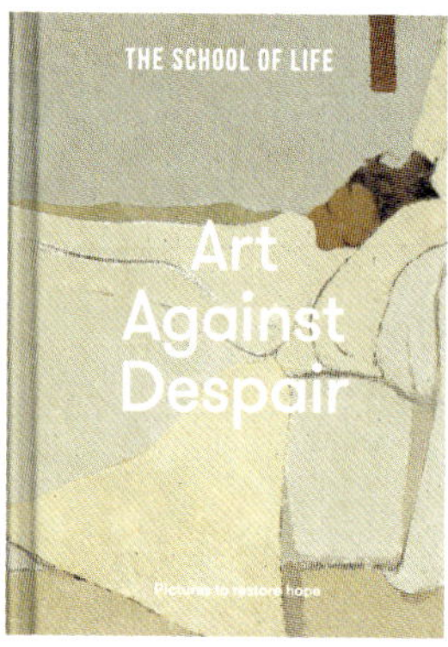

Art Against Despair

Pictures to restore hope

An inspiring selection of images offering us hope and comfort, reminding us that we are not alone in our sorrow.

One of the most unexpectedly useful things we can do when we're feeling glum or out of sorts is to look at pictures. The best works of art can lift our spirits, remind us of what we love and return perspective to our situation. A few moments in front of the right picture can rescue us.

This is a collection of the world's most consoling images, accompanied by small essays that talk about the works in a way that offers us comfort and inspiration. The images in the book range wildly across time and space: from ancient to modern art, east to west, north to south, taking in photography, painting, abstract and figurative art. All the images have been carefully chosen to help us with a particular problem we might face: a broken heart, a difficulty at work, the meanness of others, the challenges of family and friends ...

This is a portable museum dedicated to beauty and consolation, a unique book about art, which is also about psychology and healing: a true piece of art therapy.

ISBN: 978-1-912891-90-0

A Therapeutic Atlas

Destinations to inspire and enchant

A selection of unique and beautiful destinations around the world, which offer powerful new perspectives on life.

The world is full of places with an unusual power to inspire and bring us joy; they might be exceptionally beautiful, resonant with history, untouched by civilisation or rich in the right sort of memories.

This is an atlas that gathers together some of the most enchanting and reinvigorating places around the world in order to heal and captivate us. It takes us to beautiful destinations in Greece, Italy, Japan, America, Chile and Australia – to name but a few. We're taken to the tops of mountains, to solitary cliffs, elegant cities – and also to some less-expected locations.

Great travellers have always known that travelling can broaden the mind; here we see how it can also heal it. Tempting images are combined with short essays that discuss the power of particular places to help us with the difficulties of being human.

ISBN: 978-1-912891-93-1

To join The School of Life community and find out more, scan below:

The School of Life publishes a range of books on essential topics in psychological and emotional life, including relationships, parenting, friendship, careers and fulfilment. The aim is always to help us to understand ourselves better and thereby to grow calmer, less confused and more purposeful. Discover our full range of titles, including books for children, here:
www.theschooloflife.com/books

The School of Life also offers a comprehensive therapy service, which complements, and draws upon, our published works:
www.theschooloflife.com/therapy

THESCHOOLOFLIFE.COM